Carolyn S. Foote

Selected Poems

cold-drill books
State University
e, Idaho 83725

Acknowledgments

Some of these poems have appeared in *cold-drill EXTRA*.

Editors: Judith Wright, Ross Nickerson
Editor for *cold-drill books*: Tom Trusky

ISBN 0-916272-26-5

Library of Congress Catalog Card Number:
84-71629

Inscribe when you have time
These words for my epitaph:
"Damned fool, unequal to reality,
Burned out by hopeless love, rest peacefully."

Carolyn S. Foote
1975

Contents

WIDOW

WIDOW

Elizabeth, may she rest in peace,
Said "If God choose, I shall but love thee
Better after death." Did she mean his or hers?
I love my dead love, sometimes in special ways
Impossible if he were still alive;
We understood each other well, but not so well
As I now understand him. He bore his wounds
Alone, as I did mine. I regret this now;
We should have wept together, but it cheers
And lifts my spirit that he did not know
How imminent death was; he drowsed and
    slept
Until the May night took all of him away.

1975

Scavanger creatures feed
At my mental bulwarks; music I once loved
Now seems a savage blight.
So far removed from you am I that half of me
Is nothing but a hollow.
The other half
Lives dangerously on crumbs of memories
Too sparse for nourishment.

1975

Sleepless at night, I think of you asleep
In other times and places like a child
Curled warm and round against me. Let me
  keep
You a little longer someday; I am wild
With loneliness, though friends and family
Circle me with love. The light's gone out
Of all life now.
                    My friend said, "You're about
To be hurt; be careful!" Foolishly
I answered, "It is worth it," but I'm not
So sure of that; all courage drains away
On nights like this one.
                    Even when the day
Finally breaks across the east, a blot
Of emptiness enfolds my bed.
                    If you
Remain alive and cursing, send a few
Curses in this direction; all my needs
Lie in your hands; your lengthly silence feeds
Emotional disaster and despair....
For me there's no peace here nor anywhere.

                    1975

You said, "You know me so well, but I
Don't know you at all!" You're partly right
To feel a separateness; There is a night
Of utter grief between us; agony
I cannot share gnaws through my yesterdays
And my tomorrows, as it does through yours.
We cannot help each other, yet love pours
From me in floods. Your sadness flays
Me like my own...the only cure is death.
Let's bind each other's wounds as best we may;
Though we shall surely keep their scars
  forever,
We may yet find a little peace together.
Give me your hand; you are sweet life and
  breath
And tenderness, if only for one day.

                    1975

4

Write soon! Call often! I'm withering away
From lack of you. Even though a wire
Or a letter, words from you strike fire
Where all was ash before. You said,
   "Someday"
And "Next time" in the most convincing tones,
But this is wishful thinking; I know well
What burdens press on you; my state's not hell
But limbo of a nasty sort. My bones
Ache for you as I ache for my lost faith.

What use are mind and flesh that feel no peace?
What earthly good may come of separation
Cleft briefly by reunions? Every breath
I breathe is yours, and there is no release
For me in this one-way communication.

1975

Nowhere
is where we're going;
Nothing
is the thing we shall receive; and
nobody,
the friend with whom this may be shared. The
   time for us is
never; yet I'd cling to you forever
if you could let me!
Love's not negative
even when channeled into emptiness;
Accept it as you would a brief caress.

1975

5

I've never felt as close to one as far away,
Though haste and wild escape are all we've
    had.
There is a certain dignity in you
Which melts me. I'm not sure you're interested
In my reactions, but you are polite
(Or is it resigned?) to this consummate idiot
Who haunts you verbally. God knows I'd like
To do so physically instead, but this
Does not compute; life's grim demands on you
Are too many for one soul I want to give
More than you can allow.
                   Wishing is easy
But reality is hard. I'm glad to live
A few wishes in the flesh occasionally.

1975

Once, when you had drunk too much, you
    said,
"I love you." I never told you this,
Knowing the whiskey spoke to me, not you....
I'd like to hear it again; I miss
Your elfin face, your smile, your voice, your
    hands,
The magic mountaintop we visited,
Sharing sadnesses none ever understood
But you. The touch of grief brought us to bed
In ill-advised locations. I can't imagine
How fools like us survive, but I confess
My strength is growing; if there is a next time,
I'll say a lot more "No" and much less "Yes."

1975

**Signposts to hell point everywhere you're
    not;**
Long time no see, no hear, no touch, no kiss.
Sometimes imagination's safe from this,
But soon it teems with misery. I've got
Grim visions of you snockered, hurt, or dead,
Hating the vicious cycle of your work,
Curdled by all the sadnesses that lurk
Like demons round the corners of your bed.

Words are always a haven, though, for me;
I sling them out of pen onto a sheet
Of paper, where they gain a different kind
Of aspect. Fastened down with symmetry
Of rhyme and meter, they no longer beat
Like blows against my tender little mind.

1975

Night used to be for sleep; now it's a long
And eminous quietness around my bed,
Looming with longing, breathing of the dead
Beloved who once lay here pressed among
My limbs and ribs, poor, empty, sorry bones
Still flamed by fires extinguished long ago.
If God indeed took Adam's rib to grow
A woman for him, woman all alone
Should die when Adam dies; she is his part,
His warm extension, kindled by his hands,
Blessed by his glance. His blood fills up her
    heart;
His tears, her eyes; his gardens are her lands;
His children, hers. The taste of grief is tart.
Where Eden bloomed now lie vast arid sands.

1975

Intellectual emanism is easy
For victims of verbal flux:
At last I see myself objectively for a moment:
After months of useless agony,
Self tortures self no more. Illusion wanes
A little, at least.
Body, subdued at last
By re-emerging mind looks at its flesh
With tolerance, though it's impossible
To cast aside the taste of yours completely.

Bear with me, as only you know how,
Bleak vistas stretching far (so far!) ahead.
Horizons desert-empty, flat with snow,
Extend unbroken arms beyond us.
You knew it all along and tried to say so
To deaf ears.
I'm listening, now!

[1975]

Pain creeps farther every desperate day
Into the dismal channels of my mind,
Which mercifully empty for a year
Now overflows with you. Decerebrate
I'd rather be than feel this empathy
with one so far away and silent. We
Came close together in a hectic time
Of autumn air and color, water sweet
As lover's breath, a rude and stony bed,
Small shelter from the frost; camp fires
    exhaled
Their incense and their ashes on our hair.
Now their charcoal lies beneath the snow
As does my sinking spirit, all alone.
"Alone, alone, alone" runs through my veins,
Spills out my eyes, drives deep into the bone,
Stiffens the aching flesh which once was
    warmed
By yours. Pray through the wintertime
That buried fires may burn again in spring.

1974

Here lies the desiccate anatomy
Of love destroyed by words. One can do
    anything
With language, even murder! This ability
Terrifies soul and spirit. Now I bring
Abjection and apology too late
To resurrect a body dead and cold
As December sky. Jabberweek's my mate;
Mome raths my companions. I'm too old
For either, but the gibberish pours from me
Like a toxic fountain towards all that I have
    lost.

If God grant me a next time, I will be
Silent as stone, remembering the cost
Of senseless, uncontrolled verbosity.

1975

**Should you happen to be sap enough to
    wonder,**
Signs point towards inability to cope;
These two-way signs can rip a soul asunder:
One half smiles genially; the other part
Wrestles in the dark with its own needs, selfish
    and glum.
Dishonesty here breeds
Prizes well-deserved: the end of the rope
Dangles invitingly.
Disrupted heart aches like a childhood wound.

Only the sound
Of your beloved voice can heal much ill...
How I regret my promise to be still!

1976

9

My arms feel vacant as my house tonight,
Permanently, perhaps. A bit of sleep
Would do no harm; I am a quivering heap
Of emotional garbage. It's not very bright
To dwell on deprivation. How do you
Escape dismay so easily? You said
"Do what you want." I want you in my bed.
But you have also told me "Never view
The possibility of love; Don't weep!
Or I shall turn you off." God's teeth! How
Could anybody follow such instruction?
You must forgive me for the bleak deduction
That no matter what I do, I cannot keep
In touch with you for long. Goodbye for now.

1976

If you believe, as I am sure you do
That life can be compartmentalized,
You must have certain ways of shutting out
the real responses and emotions.

We can view ourselves in any role we like
Granted a bit of leeway.
I have seen myself
As lady beautiful, melting, open, needing to
give and give
To the most disenchanted man I've ever
loved.

You said "I don't want to live long," and "I love
    my wife"
And "You're so nice!"
How contradictory can you get?

I said "No strings. I won't exert emotional
    pressure on you."

Liars, both of us, though not intentionally;
My walls are broken down;
Only shreds of artificial personality remain
    here.

10

Miles and miles away
Your stubborn independence reinforces
barriers always strong.
What am I to do
With love's wellsprings, whose deepest
sources
Tear me to pieces?

It is easiest just to fall dead, but I cannot do
    this
To those who really love me.

Be blessed within those walls
That no impassioned kiss can rupture.
I'm still insane enough
To try to demolish them another day, if I'm
    allowed....
If not, signposts point, as usual: YOUR WAY!

[1976]

Questions

I speak answers
though you ask no questions

ask, ask!
all of me is yes.

[1976]

Maybe
Attacking you with verse
Is worse
Than silence.

Man was
Born with wagging tongue;
Who among
Us holds his peace?

Come closer to me,
Through me.

Hold me nearest
All of you;
The dearest
Memories I know
Began so.

1976

How much thanks
accrues from loving him?

A negative quantity
to the minus twelfth.

Some packages come
without instructions;
don't open them!

Preserve yourself.

1976

I won't expire of love, although
At times I hope I may...
Those who smear their hearts on paper
Live to write another day.

1976

Widow

Living alone
produces conditions
undreamed of before:

sudden ignitions
of strange appetite
for unsuitable food
and drink
late at night,
a penchant for letting
disorder pertain
in household and person,
a hearty disdain
for anything useful.

My mind's vacuum vacant;
if I didn't know better,
I'd think I was pregnant.

1976

Arthritis

Nine fingers stride
across the keyboard
with acceptable skill;
the tenth's a laggard.

There's no chance it will
catch up.

Bach and Buxtehude
flinch in old graves
where my dismal, crooked digit
belongs also.

I'd like to abandon it
on someone's doorsill.

1976

Dirty

I really haf
to take a baf.

1976

Sometimes I wish I hadn't learned from you
The temporary, sharp exhilaration
Of bourbon in my coffee.
                              My situation
Here lends itself to drunkenness. The view
From this empty house is just as beautiful
As it always was, but my appreciation
Deteriorates the longer I'm alone.
The impulse to perform the dutiful
Little domestic tasks dwindles; I am one
With all those hopeless souls who live on fumes
Of their respective drinks and drugs.
                              God keep
Us all in our insensibility
From starting conflagrations in our rooms
To wipe us out when we are fast asleep.

[1976]

Reflections

inspired (partly) by
Judy's Screen Door

Times passionate and frustrate beyond sense
Are not the times I miss you most.
                              The hands
Once urgent towards the aching, sweet consent
Of joining flesh could also soothe demands
From dripping faucets, choke that sticks and
        stalls,
Patchy plaster falling off the walls
U-joints leaking, wires that spit and burn,
Solenoids gone scatty.
                              How I yearn
To lead you to the bedroom, where the lamp
Blinks screwloose in its socket, to the damp
Recesses downstairs where the furnace fire
Grows feeble, to the washer and the dryer,
Both sullen in their niches!
                              My desire
For kisses still distracts me, but your skills
Could smooth away a host of other ills!

1976

15

Missing the Bushs

A Bush in the yard is worth two in McCall;
One Foote in the house is no better than none.
When you are away the glamorous glitter
Of this neighborhood leaves it; I feel that I own
A shred of the land which you strongly
    protected
From hatchets and horses, from trespassers
    (ever
crossing the ditch and trampling the flowers
of lettuces...wild ones). My every endeavor
To do the same thing gets weak as time passes;
A voice in the nighttime, young and profane,
Sounds in the yard; I wish you were home!
Wishing is easy; the truth is a pain!

1976

Wheels
Wheels
Wheels will get you nowhere;
Circuitous the wheel
And it always stays the same

I change
Every week without you
Soon you will be nothing
But a wheel
Within a wheel
Without a name.

[1976]

16

Cycle

Here
is a stain
of oil, fuel, sweat, blood...all yours
across wildflowers.

[1976]

A Toast

To skin stretched taut across unwilling bones,
To fleshy scars flavored with gasoline,
Creamy thigh, hard mouth, and all between,
Of which I never, never hold enough...
Nor ever shall.

Incalculably rough
Hastening hands whose bite is sharp as teeth,
Tendernesses lying underneath,
But heavy armored, masked; I cannot see
These but I feel them. I am much too soft
For you, and you are much too hard for me.

[1976]

Each morning, it's true,
I visualize you:
Like a trickle of acid,
You make me less placid.
While scrubbing the sink
I remember your face;
While wearing my mink,
I feel your embrace.
There ain't no excuse
To be a recluse
With nothing but you on my mind:
Obsessions neurotic
Plague this psychotic....
She doesn't know how to unwind.
If you were kinder,
You'd unwind her!

You've given me
The damnedst things;
Plastic shelter,
Wanderings
Through empty forests,
Breaking into
Houses that we
Shouldna been to,
Intimacy
Where the litter
Is collected,
(I'm not bitter....
Just astonished!)

I abhor
A dull routine:
Please give me more!

1976

18

Outpouring flames
May sink to embers of a fire asleep
But flare up hot again
In winds of metabolic change:
Sin dudo me enciendes
Y me gusta me arder, siempre, siempre...
But
The question is
Which is kindling, which the kindled fuel?
Surely a holocaust destroys at last
Combustibles which started it alight.

1976

Tentative

Under winter white
above the creek
lie campfire ashes.
Do you think
those can be set alight
when spring dissolves the snow?

If so,
give me a match,
a coffeepot,
a kiss......

Heaven will never
offer more
than this.

1976

Ladle gravy on his flapjack;
Throw your heartache in the fire;
Fold your tarp and pack your knapsack.

Bind his bedroll with barbed wire!

1977

Though other bits
of you may vex me,
I am glad
your feet are sexy.

[1977]

20

I send you, with love, sagebrushes,
ready to bloom, the hushes
of earliest morning,
skywater, earthwater, firelight,
early as youth, later than years past midnight,
thunder inflating all ears, moments of ashes
blown into eyes, as smoke they say follows
    beauty.

I send you no task, no inexorable pressure of
    duty,
nothing but cloud, storm wind-madness of
    aspens.

Linger a bit; though the swallows go
    southward,
here
is a home to remember. The shackle that
    fastens
yourself to this haven cannot be unlocked in a
    hurry.

1977

Old enough for wisdom, having known
Birth, long illnesses, the serpent's teeth
Of thankless children, wounds, dishonesty,
Stresses, frustrations, unexpected death,
And death foreseen...the latter's worse, I
think....
I'm still an open door.
              Experience
Has taught me nothing; what a waste of years
And human strength; I need a sturdy fence
Around me!
    Grief stood sixteen months between
My life and other lives; then an explosion
Of ill-considered feelings dulled its force,
Set me adrift on seas of wild emotion,
Wiped out intelligence, stranded me apart
From those who love me dearly. Now I center
All my days on you. This is idiocy
For both of us; I cannot enter
Your life, nor fold you into mine, much as I
    long
To do so. Forgive me for extending
Heart and hands to you with such abandon.
I said, "It will not hurt you," but my sending
Impassioned messages puts a strain
On you. I promise there will be no more
Of these; I'll keep them to myself,

Hoping that time and patience will restore
Me to sanity.
    Meantime, I pray
Life may be gentle with you every day.

[1977]

Empty Absence

How can an emptiness
be so full as this
full of the never kiss
never caress?

1977

My Progeny

I don't give a damn
what happens to my assets
or to my numerous progeny:
at this stage I am clinging
to the possibility
that something more
will happen
to me!

[1977]

This night's alive with luminosity,
Icy with long winds shivering the star
That hangs above my rooftop, cold and far,
But not so far away as you from me.

[1978]

Comment

Imagination pulls it all togevver;
Imagination makes it all worf wile.
     When reddy to barf
     Any biby, not arf
Your precautions will save this poor chile!

1980

PHOTOGRAPHS

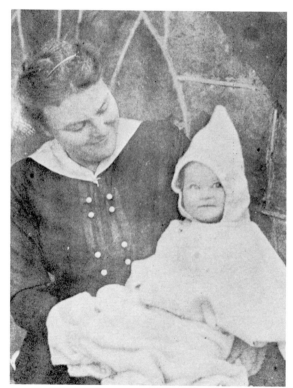

Amelia Werner Swayne and Carolyn Hope Swayne about 1919.

Carolyn Hope Swayne on her wedding day, 1 June 1940.

Carolyn and Norman Foote, 1 June 1940, wedding at Princeton.

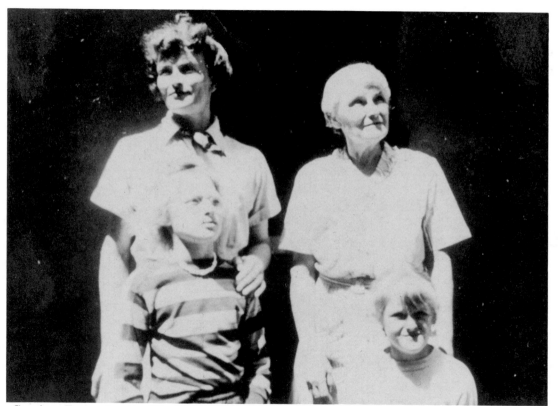

Carolyn Foote, Amelia Werner Swayne, Margaret and Judith Foote, 1948 or 1949, Newton, Pennsylvania.

27

All the Footes, Roanridge, Parkville, Missouri, 1950.

Norman and Carolyn Foote at his retirement in 1971, Boise, Idaho.

Norman Foote, 1973, Boise, Idaho.

Ennis woman, 61, dies in trailer fire

ENNIS — Carolyn H. Foote, 61, widow of Norman L. Foote, former arch deacon of the Episcopal Diocese in Helena, burned to death Wednesday in an early morning fire in her trailer house at Slide Inn near Quake Lake south of Cameron.

Roy Kitson, Madison County sheriff-coroner, was called to the scene at 7:30 a.m. He said it was 45 minutes before firefighters could extinguish the flames to recover her body. Cause of the fire is unknown.

Mrs. Foote was born May 1, 1918, in Newtown, Pa. She grew up there and attended Bernard University in New York City. In 1940, she and Mr. Foote married in the Princeton University Chapel in Princeton, N.J.

Rev. Foote was Episcopal minister in Virginia City, Sheridan and Jefferson, then moved to Helena when he became arch deacon. He directed the National Institute for the Episcopal Church in Parkville, Mo., and later was in Boise as Episcopal bishop for Idaho. Rev. Foote died May 12, 1975.

Mrs. Foote graduated in 1963 from the College of Idaho, and taught there until 1973. She moved to the Slide Inn in 1977.

Surviving are sons, Roy of Emmett, Idaho, and Ralph of Logan, Utah; daughters, Judy Schank of Boise and Margaret Harris of Portland; brother, Kingdon Swayne of Newtown; and 10 grandchildren. Services are pending in K&L Mortuary in Ennis.

Obituary, Carolyn Foote, 1980.

Metal box recovered from fire in which Carolyn Foote lost her life.

31

Sample manuscripts found in metal box.

GRANDMOTHER

Nursery Chant for Now

Aunt Rhody lives in a boxy house;
we're going there to dine
on a goose she'll roast,
tea and toast,
ices and pies
with walnut eyes,
and beakers of dewberry wine.

The box house shimmers
beside a river:
flume, spume,
flow and flood
over loam and loess,
largesse of God,
falsely fabled unlimited
blood of the land.
Flow and flood,
cradle of fishes,
washer of dishes,
stirrer of dandy
spume and foam,
disastrous drench
on less and loam.
Blood of the land
purveys a stench
of sludge and glue
for baby to bathe in;

methanous brew
for sister to wade in,
flood and flow
unlimited

Go tell Aunt Rhody the goose is dead;
fecal and foul floats her drooped, drowned
    head.

[1968]

35

For Sons

At the movie
At the concert,
Hold her harmless hand;
Stay away
From breast and thigh
Unless you understand
The Repercussions,
Consequences,
Conflagrations, which
May vex your heart
And your exchequer:
You're not all that rich!

[1968]

Grandma's Place

We like to go to grandma's place
Because we don't have to eat formal and say
    grace
We can sit on the floor
And eat onion sandwiches galore.

Grandma doesn't sew or cook
but she knows many interesting things
Because she reads so many books
She could even dance a highland fling.

If you bring a lizard, snake or mouse
Grandma doesn't get up on the chair and shout
She holds them with loving care
Then tells us how they fare.

[1975]

Unsolicited Advice

(Also Titled "A Moral (for John Updike's
'A Month of Sundays'")

If, in matters sexual,
you deem your arts effectual,
pay some heed to me;
competition
brings attrition;
there's no need to be
interminably potent
or lightning quick to get
"Into her pants" as you
so quaintly put it.

You did not invent
the act of love.

You're not beyond
responsibility;
getting in is
relatively easy;
getting out
might not be!

1976

For Margaret's Children

Hinkory dinkery dink
The skink drank up the ink
His head turned black
And he lay on his back
Upsidedown in the sink.

Hunkory dunkory dunk
This house is full of junk
The bedroom squeaks
And the bathroom leaks
And the children are covered with gunk.

Hickory dickory dock
Joseph fell on a rock
But Carolyn said:
"His foot's not dead,
It's just crawling out of its sock."

Heemery deemery deem
I had the loveliest dream
I took Carolyn's toes
and fingers and nose
And ate them with sugar and cream.

Hoofery doofery doof
The dog flew up on the roof
The firemen came round
And carried him down
While he shouted rowf rowf and woof woof.

37

Hamery damery day
While Joseph was riding away
To Grandmother's house
He ate up a mouse
And said "This tastes better than hay."

Hefery defery eet
Joseph likes cherries and meat
Carolyn eats soup
with crakers and goop
But Christopher chews on his feet.

1972

Grandchildren

All these marvels
came to be
from grandparents'
venery.

1976

On Being a Landowner

School
opens its May
spewing out children
across my flower beds;
carefree feet
knock down my sprinkler heads;
chalk marks desecrate
the tires and hubs
of my old car.
Thrown pebbles lie
concealed in grass
awaiting power mower;
they will fly
like bullets!
I have tried
ferocity and friendship.
Nothing moves them,
though undoubtedly
somebody,
somewhere in this neighborhood
loves them.

1976

Grandmas are made
Of sugar and cookies,
Pillowy bosoms,
Fat little laps
?
Not this one.
She snaps!

Grandmas all welcome
Us at the door;
When we break their dishes,
They give us some more
?
Not this one.
She's sore!

Grandmas are fragrant
With spices and herbs,
Lavander ladies
In lacy old cloaks
?
Not this one.
She smokes!

Grandmas are cuddly,
Reaching for babies,
Loving and patient.
Full of sly winks
?
Not this one.
She drinks!

Grandmas are brave
To live all alone,
Quiet and widowed
Without any mates
?
Not this one.
She dates!

1976

Tribute

In memory of all
the joys you've afforded us,
you shall have kisses
from Crotalus horridus,
pillows of Rhus
toxicodendron
to soften the seat
which you rest your end on,
hog jowls and fat back
with nettles for greens,
fleas in your shirt,
mice in your jeans.
May various leeches
adhere to your bum;
may your gut be a haven
for Dipylidum.
You shall have warts
on elbows and knees,
a dose of the pox,
Aschelminthes,
snow in July,
heat waves in winter,
pain from a terribly

infected splinter.
If that's not enough,
I'll look up some more
rude creatures and write
a friendly encore.

[1976]

Message for Bud, 12/21/78

What shall we do with the terrible Foote?
Dip her in rust and glue,
Throw her fierce cat in the river's deeps,
Chase her fool men over lover's leaps,
Foul up her phone with snarls and beeps,
Dismantle her big Ski-Doo.

Mash up her merriment, spoil her tea
With essence of skunk. Eccentricity
Deserves to be punished; Come with me
To stow a dead mouse in her shoe.

Sneer at the subtleties of her wit,
Bury her deep in the garbage pit,
This is the only way to git
Some peace, which is surely due.

In after years when the blizzards roll
Across the steam from the garbage hole,
We shall think of the Foote that lost her soul
And commend her to compost. Phew!

1978

Kripling Seethes Again

When your hair has turned to silver,
I shall hate you, just as now;
When your strength is gone forever,
I shall beat you anyhow.

As your teeth and eyes grow dimmer,
I'll point out these things to you;
You're not getting any slimmer;
Your lips are turning blue.

If you socks be stinking rotten,
I will fing them to the flames;
Should you stagger home besotten,
I'd still call you nasty names.

Let us wander through the meadow
Where the steer manure lies...
I shall press your filthy shadow
Into numerous cow pies!

1979

WRITER

Invocation

The grey roads stretch to north and south; they
    wind
On bare, brown hills, unfriendly and unkind.
The cold wind whimpers through the starving
    air,
Hungry for warmth and color, but the bare
Brown hills lift dull breasts to the aching sky,
Piled up with dark-bruised cloudbanks, riding
    high
And cold astride the empty, seeking wind.
Dark tree-hands rake the air; two dead leaves,
    pinned
Upon a gnarled finger make small song
Together, dryly crackling. Fog-gray, long
Thin rivers fork beyond the frozen trees
And disappear in distance. Dead elm sees
Dead elm in their snow-flowing quietness.
Grey silence lengthens. If a god possess
This bleakness with its barren fields of cold,
Let him remember, ere the year is old,
To fleece bare brown with white, to shorten
    slow
Gray nights with silver glistening of snow.

[1934]

Search Out Windy Places

You sluggards...you who lie all day abed,
Curled up in musty contemplation, there
Above the swarming streets in upblown dust
Of needless hurrying...You, you who rust
The cup of Wisdom in this rotting air,
And trample Beauty with your listless tread,
Unleash your soul...search out a windy place.
Throw off the chains that hold you, find your
    wings
And, in the freedom that your new hope brings,
Stand up and meet tomorrow face to face.

[1934]

**When I am dead and voiceless winds sweep
    sadly**
Above my lonely grave,
Where stars go down to meet the water,
    jeweled
in every wave.

I shall have lost the blossoms of my sorrow
I cherished to life's close,
And in my fleshless fingers hold one flower,
Your friendship's rose.

1934

Rondeau

Forget my grave; I will not know
If aimless west winds toss the snow
In tattered shreds of frozen lace
Upon my silent resting place,
When I have tasted earth below.
When lonely winter sunsets throw
Their fading, ashen afterglow
Beyond the mountain's wrinkled face,
Forget my grave.
Above my still lips, marching slow,
The footsteps of the hours go,
Majestically, with royal grace,
Each in its own appointed space.
If you should weep, I would not know...
Forget my grave.

1934

To H.R.

I put my silly love for you away;
I half forgot your tangled mop of hair,
The crumpled, wrinkled suit you used to wear,
Your restless mouth, the tantalizing way
A smile played with the corners of your eyes.
I blurred all these things; and then, tonight,
I saw your blond hair glint beneath a light
And hear you tell the same, familiar lies.

I took my dead love from her hiding place;
I dressed her dusty bones in gold and red,
And gloated on your half-remembered face.
I watched the old expressions play, and then
I put away my love, for she is dead;
Tomorrow, I shall bury her again.

[1936]

Drowning in a sea
of estrogens, injested orally
the female of the species, on the prowl,
sobs in the nighttime,
paints her eyelids green,
eschews the sunlight.

Now she crawls
across the private chamber, quadruped.

She'll be stiff, one way or another,
before the cocktail hour.

1968

Circle

Devising poetry
is wallowing
in one's own infirmity.

[1975]

French Dressing

Like oil and vinegar,
we're not too easy to combine...
what ends are you pursuing
when you're not pursuing mine?

1976

Affair

Relationships
like this may fail
when all that they include
is tail.

1976

Life seldom brings
the happy chance
of catching you
without your pants.

1976

Linda fishes very well;
She has a lot of lures.
I've a few of those myself,
But not so good as hers!

1976

A Modern Andrew Marvell Might Have Written

Lady, lady, can you love me,
Clasp, envelop fragments of me,
In your depths of velvet glove me?
Do it, do it, do it!

Though I've known you just a week
All my inhibitions leak;
Lady, lady, cheek to cheek,
Do it, do it, do it!

Hot as atom, split, enclose me;
(Can't imagine why you chose me;
Once a female almost froze me.)
Do it, do it, do it!

Cloister's chill can't satisfy;
Lie with me; all liquid, lie!
Give St. Paul the evil eye.
Do it, do it, do it!

With your body I'm obsessed;
Let me taste the luscious breast;
God's sake, woman, get undressed!
Do it, damn it, do it!

1978

[Limericks]

Just after a certain event
A delectable, fair penitent
Confessed to her priest.
Not shocked in the least,
He's now happily paying her rent.

When Dorothy Parker had need
Of pets, she brought home birds to feed;
She named them all Onan
Because they had thrown on
The cage bottom all of their seed.

Although I sporadically try
To catch trout, I am living a lie:
The thing I most wish for
And really would fish for
Is an angler who's broken his fly.

You may flinch at the lady who scored 'em;
Night after night she adored 'em.
As she writhed in the hay,
She felt, she would say,
That whoredom is better than boredom.

Pray now for desperate Myrtle,
Who contrived to make love to a turtle;
He snapped shut his shell;
With a scream, Myrtle fell.
Now there's no way she'll ever be fertile.

When he finally decided to bare it,
He revealed a device of such merit
That the ladies all shouted,
Except one, who pouted,
"Please girls, let us share it, not scare it."

The spouse of a Bishop's a lass
Of highly superior class;
So much for her worth...
She has to give birth
To sons of Bishops, alas!

It's easy for me to concede
I have feelings of passionate need:
My love is a botanist,
And he's the rottenest
Lover who ever sowed seed.

RE: 27 January

Hatchety ratchety,
Willard's a marvelous
Doubler of dactyly,
Never the fool.

****

Logophilistically
May he forever see
Language as playthings, and
Not as a tool.

[1979]

Gribbleglootch

Now hear a cheer for scruddleblutch,
For shrinks this year, though they're not much,
For gribbleglootch plus plenty hootch,
For dancing, specially the cootch.

We'll bite again the old owl's glerb
And bash him in his oohgly verb;
Beneath the yolk egg we'll hide
And snammer him on his backside!

"Twits" are great; you known it's true,
But let's leave out the double U.
Grits in such a scheme makes "gits";
Flits meanders into "fits";
Grander now in "gander" later;
Cater started out as "crater".

Spelling backwards sometimes pleases
If you relish such diseases.
Try the roadsigns: *Timil deeps.*
Gnikrap on. The driver sleeps
Through these, but he must change his tune
For *ereh yap* and *pots* quite soon.

O *yekrut ap* I ate such *feeb*
With salad made of pickled *steeb*.

Now that's enough...too much, I think...
OOH-Dark, HOO-Krad; buy me a drink!

1979

Ohne Deine Amor

Me falta immer deine Lieb;
Porqué kommst nicht aquí?
Kein Himmel Scheint; kein pájaro
Fliegt Wann du bleibst alli.

Joyas como flores raras,
Y Köngsessen möcht Ich bringen...
Lieb und Treu nach tigo siempre...
Sin dich ningun puede singen.

Wäre besser wenn la muerte
Me permitiera schlafen.
Vielgeliebte, meine puerta
Immer wartet, abierta.

1980

Ohne Deine Amor

Translation
(By Willard Espy)

The loss of love's perhaps least loss of all—
A raindrop stolen from a brimful sea.
Why stars should cease to shine, and birds to
call,
Must puzzle you—I know it puzzles me.

I offered flow'rs like gems; you, gems like
flow'rs;
I, manna; you, the milk of paradise.
(Mere idle promises in idle hours:
Their unfulfillment comes as no surprise.)

I wonder...is your latch undrawn tonight
As mine is? Is your night-lamp by the bed?...
We shall sleep better, when we've snuffed the
light...
When we are dead, are dead, are dead, are
dead.

1980

Typescript, microfilm and 35 mm slide copies of the poems contained in this volume are available at the Boise State University Library which also is the repository for the original manuscripts, which comprise this volume, and other works by Foote.

Publication of this book was only possible because of Ross Nickerson's insight and wit.

NOTES
by Judith Foote Wright

Carolyn Foote's poems are reproduced verbatim in this volume.
Dates and information in brackets have been supplied by Judith R. F. Wright.

Page

3 **Elizabeth, may she rest in peace,**
Elizabeth Barrett Browning.
Norman L. Foote died 12 May 1974.

3 **Scavanger creatures feed**
The epitaph on the frontispiece was written below this poem in the original manuscript of Foote's works and scratched out by her.

7 **Night used to be for sleep; now it's a long**
Eminous - outstanding, remarkable.

9 **Here lies the desiccate anatomy**
Jabberweek - "jabberwocky"
Mome raths - "momerath"
Foote is playing with words from Lewis Carroll.

14 **Arthritis**
Foote had degenerative arthritis which destroyed the discs in her back and also her thumb joints. She had a steel rod in her back and plastic thumb joints. She made herself play the organ every day to keep her hands moving.

15 **Reflections inspired (partly) by Judy's Screen Door**
Judy - Judith R. F. Wright, her daughter.

16 **Missing the Bushs**
Claire Bush and family, vacationing in McCall, Idaho, were Foote's neighbors when the latter lived on McMullen in Boise, Idaho.

19 **Outpouring flames**
"Sin dudo me enciendes
Y me gusta me arder, siempre, siempre..."
Without a doubt you make me red hot
And I love to burn, always, always...
(Translation: Dr. Juan Savaugeau)

23 **My Progeny**
Foote had 4 children, 10 grandchildren and 7 step-grandchildren.

35 Nursery Chant for Now
Aunt Rhody - from the folksong "Go Tell Aunt Rhody" (her favorite rendition was by Burl Ives).

36 For Sons
Foote's Sons - LeRoy Francis Foote and Ralph Norman Foote.

37 Unsolicited Advice
Foote corresponded with John Updike, author of many books (including *A Month of Sundays*), and with Willard Espy, author of many books (including *Words at Play*, *Almanac*, *Oysterville*, and *Almanac II*).

In her youth Foote met many famous authors. She wrote in 1980 to Willard Espy:
Every week Friday or Saturday night, we had cultural or dramatic or musical performances in a large auditorium. Attendance was voluntary. Great poets came to recite their works: Frost, Markham, Sandburg, for example. But the one that brought the house down and doubled the attendance on subsequent visits was T. A. Daly.

37 For Margaret's Children
Margaret Harris, Foote's oldest daughter. Her children mentioned in the poem were Joseph and Carolyn. Christopher is the children's dog.

38 Grandchildren
See note for page 23.

40 Tribute
Rhus toxicodendron - poison ivy
Dipylidum - dog/cat tapeworm
Aschelminthes - roundworm
pox - syphilis

41 Message for Bud, 12/21/78
Bud Neis, Foote's landlord and friend at Slide Inn, Cameron, Montana.

42 Kripling Seethes Again
Foote often signed her poems "Rudyard Kripling."

46 When I am dead and voiceless winds sweep sadly
Handwritten note on the bottom of this poem written by Foote long after it was written:

How cliche' can you get?

46 Rondeau
Handwritten note on the bottom of this poem written by Foote long after it was written:

!!!!!ICK!!!!

47 To H.R.
Handwritten note on the botton of this poem written by Foote long after it was written:

Very sad early crush (truly traumatic) on most promising (literary wise) classmate: ...in 1962 he was a boozy bum living with a lady(?) [in a] saloon.

49 Linda fishes very well;
Linda Bush - see note for page 16.

51 RE: 27 January
Willard - Willard Espy - see note for page 37.

53 Ohne Deine Amor Translation
Translated by Willard Espy and printed in his book *Almanac II*. It is reprinted here with his consent and blessing.

FOOTENOTES
by Judith Foote Wright

FACTS
Carolyn Hope Swayne was born May 1, 1918 at George School in Newtown, Pennsylvania, the only daughter of Norman W. Swayne and Amelia Swayne. She had four younger brothers, Kingdom, Kenneth, Philip and Malcom.

Norman W. Swayne was a chemistry teacher and tennis coach at George School, which is a Quaker boarding school. Amelia was a homemaker and very active in Quaker charity functions. Both were extremely well educated and took great pride in their education.

Carolyn Hope Swayne graduated from George School at the age of 16, went to Barnard College until sometime in 1938 or 1939 when she was in serious academic trouble and on probation. Against her family's desires she went to New York City where she lived, taught ballroom dancing and wrote verse for greeting cards. It was here she met my father, Norman L. Foote, a student at General Theological Seminary and they were married June 1, 1940 shortly after his graduation.

Subsequent to their marriage they traveled across the country to Virginia City, Montana where my father was in charge of several Episcopal missions. While they were in Virginia City my sister, Margaret, was born on May 12, 1941. In 1943 my father was appointed the Archdeacon of the Episcopal Diocese of Montana and they moved to Helena, Montana. During their time in Montana, they had three more children: myself, born September 10, 1944; LeRoy Francis, born March 19, 1949; and Ralph Norman, born April 1, 1950.

In 1950 my father became the director of the National Town & Country Institute located outside of Parkville, Missouri. The Institute was a training facility for Episcopal seminary students to learn the problems of rural life by managing and running a farm. My father ran the institute and the farm and conducted seminars. My mother herded four children and various animals.

In 1957 my father was elected the Episcopal Bishop of Idaho. Finding all of her children in school and not being interested in being a Bishop's wife, my mother went back to college. She graduated from the College of Idaho, in Caldwell, Idaho in 1963. After graduation she worked full-time (being paid part-time wages) and taught various courses in the Biology Department at the College of Idaho under the direction of Lyle Stanford who was the chairman of the department. After Lyle Stanford's death the college did not request her return.

In 1972 my father retired and on May 12, 1974 he died of congestive heart failure. Following his death, my mother lived in Boise until 1977 when she moved to Cameron, Montana and she died there in a fire in 1980.

MORE IMPORTANT FACTS

Animals

We always had dogs and cats but it was in Missouri that my mother began acquiring birds. First it was parakeets that provided food for various cats. We then had a baby grackle, fallen from its nest, who thought he was one of my mother's children. He finally succumbed to a cat as well. Then one day my mother was shopping in Kansas City and went into a Katz Drug Store. There in the liquor department advertising Old Crow whiskey was a raven. He was for sale probably because had learned to scream "Help. Police. Let me out!" Along with the bird, whose name was Ronnie, my mother purchased a bottle of scotch for my father. For many years with each bird she brought home, my mother also brought home a bottle of scotch.

Ronnie was part of our family until the early 1970's when he disappeared in Montana. He had a vocabulary of hundreds of words and sounds. Able to change his tone of voice, he was often mistaken for my father. He went on trips and vacations with us and it was not unusual for my mother to drive through the countryside with four children, two dogs, several cats and Ronnie.

In later years she traveled with a parrot (Simon) and a macaw (Tonto) as well.

Her interest in pets included both warm and cold blooded animals. We often had tarantulas, spiders and snakes. During her days as a student at the College of Idaho we acquired barn owls and magpies and on one occasion a mynah bird. We were also blessed with very cold-blooded beasts: dead sharks and cats which fell from the freezer to your feet if you were not careful opening the door.

Bishop's Wife

The traditional function of a Bishop's wife is to oversee female church functions, such as teas and dinners, accompany the Bishop as he travels, keep a showplace house for the expected important visitor and generally be a shadow of the Bishop. Mrs. Foote did not fall into any of these categories and the Bishop did not mind a bit.

When we first arrived in Idaho we moved into the "Bishop's House" which was then located on 2nd and Idaho Streets in Boise. The previous residents had painted the entire house red and green. My mother proceeded to redo the interior and set up housekeeping. After the remodeling she found her life lacking and attempted to fulfill the traditional role of Bishop's wife. She tried pouring for tea when requested, but far too often became engrossed in bird-watching and forgot her tea-time duties.

Once she decided it would be appropriate to have various local dignitaries for dinner. The house was cleaned to a shine, the meal prepared and the dining room table filled with china and crystal. However the guests ate dinner on a bare table with plastic plates because Ronnie, whose cage was next to the table in the dining room, had decided to bathe just prior to the beginning of the meal. This dinner concluded her days as a "Bishop's Wife" and the only church functions she attended thereafter were special occasions such as ordinations and meetings of a church guild, which consisted of ladies who preferred scotch in their teacups instead of tea.

Having decided a "Bishop's Wife's" life was not her cup of tea, she enrolled as a student at College of Idaho and began to pursue a degree. She graduated in 1963 one week before I graduated from high school. Following her graduation she avoided churchly duties by giving her full attention to being a teacher.

Professor Foote

Lyle Stanford was the head of the Biology Department for the College of Idaho at the time my mother started her career as a student. They developed a close friendship and upon her graduation he asked if she could work part-time for him assisting him with biology labs. She went right to work.

My mother began her teaching career assisting Dr. Stanford, but it progressed to teaching biology, comparative anatomy and various other courses. She was never paid more than a part-time salary but she worked eight to ten hours a day and supervised field trips to Baja, California, the San Juan Islands and Mexico. Her extra hours were spent preparing for her clases with special aids for study such as poems about the brain or various other parts of the anatomy. Students visiting our house with their problems was not unusual. It was also not unusual for her to help her students smuggle crawly things from California and Mexico by placing them in her sleeping bag or in the door of her car.

Unfortunately for her students, when Lyle Stanford died, the College did not request her return. She missed her teaching very much; however, I am sure the snake and tarantula populations of Mexico sighed with relief.

Widowhood

For many years my mother suffered from back pain and underwent the usual cures for this ailment which ranged from hysterectomy to much medication. She rarely sat in a chair and it was not unusual for her to lie on the floor to read, talk or write. In April of 1974 she was informed that she had a degenerative form of arthritis which had destroyed the discs in her back. She was given the choice of having her back fused or undergoing surgery which would place a steel rod in her back to support her spine. She chose the rod. It was an extremely painful and traumatic surgery and left her in a body cast for nearly nine months.

A few days prior to the time my mother was due home from the hospital my father became aware that his health was deteriorating fast. He had emphysema and knew the symptoms of congestive heart failure. He had the house repainted, instructed me in their financial affairs and drove himself to Cascade to the care of his doctor. My mother came home from the hospital and two days later my father died.

There is no way to comprehend what trauma she endured following his death and her surgery. To further complicate her stress, her brother, Philip, died unexpectedly shortly after my father's death. She had already lost two of her other brothers, so now only she and her brother, Kingdom, of five Swayne children survived. Somehow she survived the hot months in a cast, and the loneliness of not only losing my father but also discovering that friends of the Bishop are not always friends of the family.

My mother and father had spent every August for many years on Cliff Lake near the Idaho-Montana border and in 1975 she returned there for the whole summer. She found herself recoving. She rode horses again, fished, painted and wrote poetry. She found the companionship of a gentleman and discovered a new world.

During the summers of 1975 to 1977, when she finally moved to Montana permanently, she discovered many new things. Among them were staying out all night in bars, riding motorcycles and mastering the art of snowmobiling. She danced, caroused and was generally unseemly— and loved those moments the most. The rest of her time was lonely and she often drank too much or played too many sad songs on her organ.

She lived in a trailer at a resort called "The Slide Inn" just south of Earthquake Lake outside of Yellowstone Park from 1977 to 1980. Her only neighbors for miles were the Neis family who owned the Inn. In summer many people came and went and she made many friends and many more acquaintances. During the winter her companions were elk, deer, many birds and snow and more snow. She rode her snowmobile with the help of the Neises and enjoyed it immensely. The Neis' favorite memories of her are related to her poetry. She never forgot a birthday or other occasion and marked each with a poem.

In April of 1980 in the early hours of the morning her trailer caught fire and burned so rapidly that the Neises were unable to rescue her from the flames.

The Box

After the death of my mother, my sister, Margaret, and brother Roy, and I flew to the snow of Montana to settle her affairs. The only possessions that had escaped the fire were her car and her snowmobile. The rest was a large snowcovered pile of ashes. My sister, who had never been to Slide Inn, was compelled to explore the ashes. During the exploration a metal box was discovered which contained the majority of my mother's poems and other writings which she had saved from the time she was a girl. Some were burned beyond recognition from the heat of the fire; others, fortunately, were not. It is from that box and from friends who saved her writings that I have been able to reproduce her work.

Heirs and Devisees

My sister, Margaret, has three children and lives in Portland, Oregon. She has just recently separated from her husband and is learning the life of a single parent. She teaches piano and plays the organ. My brother, Roy, is an engineer for Hewlett-Packard, and with his new bride, Paula, enjoys his four children and has a tremendous amount of energy which never seems to stop. Ralph teaches at Treasure Valley Community College in Ontario, Oregon, and lives in

Fruitland, Idaho with his new wife, six of her seven sons and his son from a previous marriage. Ralph has inherited his mother's animal affinity and has numerous snakes, birds, dogs and cats. My daughter Samantha and I live in Boise with 2 dogs and various cats. Due to a trust my mother left for me, I am able, like her, to attempt to complete my college education and eat at the same time. When I am not at school I type furiously for a small group of lawyers.

Judith R. F. Wright
June, 1984
Boise

DATE DUE

PRINTED IN U.S.A.